REALITY OF THE RESURRECTION

Ross Thompson

Published by Ross Thompson, 2018.

While every precaution has been taken in the preparation of this book, the publisher assumes no responsibility for errors or omissions, or for damages resulting from the use of the information contained herein.

REALITY OF THE RESURRECTION

First edition. October 30, 2018.

Copyright © 2018 Ross Thompson.

Written by Ross Thompson.

CONTENTS

1 Reality of the Resurrection
2 No Resurrection No Salvation
3 The Resurrection destroyed the devil
4 Sometime or all the time
5 Jesus Leadership example
6 Do we struggle for holiness
7 Magnifying glass on Romans 7
8 Keeping your marriage alive
9 Developing Godly character in children
10 Interpreting 1 John
11 Jesus on men looking at women
12 Jesus had coffee with sinners
13 We win in Him
About the author

REALITY OF THE RESURRECTION

Recently I read an account of Smith Wigglesworth proving the reality of the resurrection of Jesus. He had an invitation to a gathering of friends of a man who had died. It was not the funeral. The body was in a side room behind two closed glass doors - in an open coffin. The guests gathered in a large main room. On arrival Wigglesworth walked through the gathered group looking at everybody but not saying a word. He reached the glass doors, opened them and walked up to the coffin. He took hold of the clothing of the corpse, hauled the body out of the coffin and stood it against a wall. He stood back a few steps and said, "In the name of Jesus I command you to walk." The body slid slowly down the wall to the floor. Wigglesworth picked it up and stood it against the wall. Again, he said, "I command you to walk in the name of Jesus." The body slid slowly down the wall to the floor. He stood the body against the wall a third time and witnesses said this time he roared, "I command you to walk in the name of Jesus." The dead man's eyes fluttered open and he staggered forward. Witnesses said a short time later the resurrected man and Smith Wigglesworth walked arm in arm through the astonished group.

For those people present it was no doubt a life changing event. You would not have been able to go on with 'life as usual' after witnessing such a spectacle. As ripples spread in a lake when a stone is thrown into it, the aftermath of the dead man alive again must have impacted many people. His family when he walked back into his house – the neighbours once the news reached them – his extended family – his workmates. If he turned up for work the next day that would have been something to see. When you think about it that one act of faith must have influenced a multitude of people. We can think, "Isn't that wonderful – wasn't Wigglesworth a great man of faith". We should be alert to the fact you and I have a commandment – a commandment not a suggestion – to do the very same thing. Jesus sent the twelve disciples out on an evangelistic outreach. (Mathew 10:5-8) "These twelve Jesus sent out and commanded them saying, do not go into the way of the Gentiles and do not enter a city of the Samaritans. But go rather to the lost sheep of the house of Israel. And as you go preach, saying, the kingdom of heaven is at hand. Heal the sick, cleanse the lepers, raise the dead, cast out demons. Freely you have received, freely give."

Of that verse some have said, "That was for the twelve disciples not us." If we go to the end of the book of Mathew we read; "And Jesus came and spoke to them saying, All authority has been given to Me in heaven and on earth. Go therefore and make disciples of all the nations. Baptizing them in the name of the Father and of the Son and of the Holy Spirit. **Teaching them to observe all things that I have commanded you;** and lo, I am with you always, even to the end of the age." (Mathew 28;18-20) We as Christians – and I am reminding myself here – need to be alert that we must not drift into "Having the appearance of godliness but denying it's power." (2 Tim 3:5) If we say we are disciples of Christ these things are part of our job description. Our responsibility is to be available and ready to act. If you are thinking, 'Oh I could never do that.' It's good to remind ourselves that. "You have died, and your life is hidden with Christ in God." (Col 3:3)

I heartily recommend the online Christian film 'Dead Raiser' if you have not yet come across it. The off shoot of that documentary made by a group of young Christian leaders was the DRT – Dead Raising Teams Ministry. Tyler Johnson of www.oneglance.org[1] and www.deadraisingteam.com[2] - one of those young men, has been called to make the

---

1. http://www.oneglance.org
2. http://www.deadraisingteam.com

body of Christ aware of this part of our responsibility. His book, 'How to Raise the Dead' is available at booksellers. The Lord graciously raises up people to direct our attention to what is in every one of our Bibles.

The new Testament has a dead raising event that is far more spectacular than any of Wigglesworth's raisings. "And Jesus cried out again with a loud voice and yielded up His spirit. Then behold, the veil of the Temple was torn in two from top to bottom: and the earth quaked, and the rocks split, and the graves opened; and many bodies of the saints who had fallen asleep were raised; and coming out of the graves after His resurrection, they went into the holy city and appeared to many." (Mathew 27:50-53) I think this event is a display of Gods eagerness to show the results of Jesus sacrifice of Himself and His resurrection. It seems to be a preliminary to the final resurrection mentioned by Paul in 1Corinthians 15:52. "...In a moment, in the twinkling of an eye, at the last trumpet. For the trumpet will sound, and the dead will be raised incorruptible, and we shall be changed..." It is as if God is saying, "Look here is proof of your salvation."

Imagine you were walking past one of Jerusalem's cemeteries at the very moment this happened. Graves were open, and the occupants began to climb out and walk around. Then as you watched they headed towards the cemetery gate and made for various parts of the city. If you were brave enough and decided to follow some of them, you would have seen them knocking on doors around the city and looked on as astonished residents opened their doors to find a long dead relative or friend standing there very much alive. Former acquaintances would have seen them passing and thought, "that looks like Moshe – no it can't be..." The word would have spread rapidly throughout the city because the verse tells us 'many'of the bodies of the saints were raised and appeared to 'many'. I think long afterwards those open graves would have been a witness in themselves. Many who had known those who had died and now lived, would see those open tombs and remember the death of that person whose grave was now empty.

A lot of questions come to mind when I read the verse. Some of the verse happened when Jesus was on the cross and cried out – the rest of it happened after His resurrection. When Jesus yielded up His spirit the earth quaked, rocks split, and the bodies of the saints were raised. It wasn't until after His resurrection they came out of the graves and went into the city. It seems they were raised but lay in their graves until Christs resurrection on the third day. Did the resurrected ones continue to live in Jerusalem or were they taken to heaven? Who were these raised saints? Were they well known Old Testament characters? Was John the Baptist among them? God certainly chose a remarkable way to advertise the truth of Jesus salvation.

There is no doubt the power of God in our lives is the proof of the resurrection. Jesus commandment to the twelve after His resurrection was to wait until they had received power from the Holy Spirit. They would then have equipping as witnesses of the living Christ.

Jesus as the first born from the dead destroyed the devil who had the power of death through sin. Christ showed Himself to be the holy Son of God by His resurrection from the dead. In Him, the same power that raised Jesus from the dead is in our lives. Our call is to show that power as proof of the reality of the Gospel. (Rev1:5) (Heb 2:14) (Rom 1:4) (Ephes1:19,20) (Rom 15:19)

NO RESURRECTION NO SALVATION

"And if Christ is not risen, your faith is futile; you are still in your sins!" (1Cor 15:17) There is no salvation says Paul, without the resurrection of Jesus. Whenever salvation is explained we don't often hear "You are saved by the resurrection of Jesus Christ." Other parts of the New Testament support Pauls comment. "...that if you confess with your mouth the Lord Jesus and believe in your heart that God has raised Him from the dead, you will be saved." (Romans 10:9) Most of my Christian life I have wondered why that verse in Romans doesn't say, "...if you believe Jesus died for your sins you will be saved." The context of the passage is the basic preaching of the gospel – the first teaching an unsaved person hears from the mouth of the preacher. Why is the resurrection of Jesus important enough to be the first message given to sinners?

I think I have the answer. Christs rising from the dead proved He was the sinless Son of God. The first chapter of Romans says, "...and as to His divine nature according to the Spirit of holiness was openly designated to be the Son of God with power in a triumphant and miraculous way by His resurrection from the dead: Jesus Christ our Lord." (Ampl. Rom 1:4) The verse is saying Jesus resurrection from the dead declared openly to all, He was the Son of God with a holy divine nature. He had never sinned, and death could not hold Him. If He had not come back from the dead, it would mean He was just an ordinary man still in the grip of death like all other men. All are sinners and "...the sting of death is sin." (1 Cor 15:56) "Therefore, just as through one man, sin entered the world, and death through sin, and thus death spread to all men, because all sinned." (Rom 5: 12) Though Jesus became sin on our behalf He had never sinned personally and remained innocent and holy. He was the sin bearer who had never sinned and for that reason death and the devil had no power to hold Him.

The Bible tells us the devil had the power of death because of sin. "The wages of sin is death." (Rom 6:23) Christ took that power away from the devil because He paid for our sins with His sacrifice and returned to life as one over whom death had no power. "In as much then as the children have partaken of flesh and blood, He Himself likewise shared in the same, that through death He might destroy him who had the power of death, that is, the devil, and release those who through fear of death were all their lifetime subject to bondage." (Heb 2:14) We now understand why Paul says, ..."and if Christ is not risen, then our preaching is empty and your faith is also empty: yes and we are found false witnesses of God, because we have testified of God that He raised up Christ, who He did not raise up – if in fact the dead do not rise . For if the dead do not rise, then Christ is not risen. And if Christ is not risen, your faith is futile: you are still in your sins!" (1Cor 15:14-17

Pauls goes on to say the wonderful truth is Christ has risen from the dead - our faith is not in vain - we are not of the company of those who perish – the hardships we experience because of the preaching of the gospel are not meaningless. Jesus is the first fruits of those who have fallen asleep. A graveyard has two groups of occupants. Those who are dead and those who are asleep. Those who passed away believing are merely asleep. In speaking to the twelve about the passing of Lazarus Jesus said, "Our friend Lazarus sleeps, but I go that I may wake him." (John 11:11) Verse 43 of this chapter tells us Christ, "...cried with a loud voice, 'Lazarus come forth." The loud voice was to awaken the sleeper. At a certain time in the future a trumpet from heaven will sound – and the voice of an archangel – the Lord Himself will descend from heaven with a shout – and because of the noise all those who sleep will awaken and begin to rise. (1Thess 4:16,17)

"For I do not want you to be ignorant, brethren, concerning those who have fallen asleep, lest you sorrow as others who have no hope. For if we believe that Jesus died and rose again, even so God will bring with Him those who sleep in Jesus. For this we say to you by the word of the Lord, that we who are alive and remain until the coming of the Lord will by no means precede those who are asleep." (1Thess 4:13-15) Again Paul says our faith rests in the truth that Jesus died and rose again. Passing away with faith in that message means you will sleep waiting for the awakening call.

In reminding the Corinthian believers about the facts of the gospel, Paul puts emphasis upon the resurrection of Jesus and the fact many saw Him after He rose. "Moreover, brethren I declare to you the gospel which I preached to you, which also you received and in which you stand, by which you are also saved, if you hold fast to that word which I preached to you – unless you believed in vain. For I delivered to you first of all that which I also received; that Christ died for our sins according to the Scriptures, and that He was buried, and that He rose again the third day according to the Scriptures, and that He was seen by Cephas, and then by the twelve. After that He was seen by over five hundred brethren at once, of whom the greater part remain to the present, but some have fallen asleep. After that He was seen by James, and by all the apostles. Then last of all He was seen by me also, as by one born out of due time." (1Cor 15: 1-8) A long list of those who saw the risen Jesus underscores the importance of the reality of the resurrection as a major part of Pauls message of faith.

No wonder we are to rejoice in the Lord always regardless of our circumstances in this life. With the Prophets we say, "Death is swallowed up in victory". "O Death where is your sting?" "O Hades where is your victory?" – "The sting of death is sin, and the strength of sin is the law. But thanks be to God, who gives us the victory through our Lord Jesus Christ." (1Cor 15: 54-57) Because of the resurrection of Jesus we will be there when He puts an end to all rule and authority and power and delivers the kingdom to God His Father. We will be there having been changed - now bearing the image of the Man of heaven – with bodies raised in power, incorruptible, spiritual, immortal and ablaze with glory. (1 Cor 15:42-53)

THE RESURRECTION DESTROYED THE DEVIL

"In as much then as the children have partaken of flesh and blood. He Himself likewise shared in the same, that through death He might destroy him who had the power of death, that is, the devil." (Heb 2:14)

"He who sins is of the devil, for the devil has sinned from the beginning. For this purpose, the Son of God was manifested, that He might destroy the works of the devil." (1John 3:8)

"Therefore, He says; 'When He ascended on high, He led captivity captive, and gave gifts to men'. Now this, 'He ascended', what does it mean but that He also first descended into the lower parts of the earth? He who descended is also the one who ascended, far above all the heavens, that He might fill all things." (Ephes 4:8-10) This verse is a direct quote from Psalm 68:18 and reminds us how much of the New Testament is in the Old. This Psalm gives a wider explanation of Christs destruction of His (and our) enemies by His resurrection from the dead.

"You have ascended on high, you have led away captivity captive; You have received gifts among men, even from the rebellious also, that the Lord may dwell there. Blessed be the Lord, who bares our burden day by day, the God who is our salvation! Selah God is to us a God of acts of salvation; and to God the Lord belong escapes from death – setting us free. Surely God will shatter the head of His enemies, the hairy scalp of one who goes on in his guilty ways. The Lord said, I will bring your enemies back from Bashan; I will bring them back from the depths of the Sea, that your foot may crush them in blood..." (Psalm 68:18-22) Here we read the result of the Lord ascending on high and leading captivity captive is that the Lord may dwell among men. He carried our burden of sin and captivity to death, upon Himself. He is to us a God who has done acts of salvation and allowed us to escape from death through Him. Escape is in the plural here referring to the many who will escape from death by receiving Jesus as saviour. The reference to the Lord destroying His enemies by shattering their head and crushing them with His foot brings to mind Gods prophecy of Genesis 3:15 " (to the serpent) And I will put enmity between you and the woman, and between your seed and her Seed; He shall bruise your head, and you shall bruise His heel."

Ephesians 4:8 in the Amplified Bible says, when Jesus ascended "He led a train of vanquished foes." What does that mean – "He led captivity captive". His ascension is Christs resurrection from the dead. The vanquished foes and captivity are the devil and his minions. Adam and Eves disobedience to Gods command in the garden handed us (humanity) over to death. "But of the tree of the knowledge of good and evil you shall not eat, for in the day you eat of it you shall surely die." (Gen 2:17) "Therefore, just as through one man, sin entered the world, and death through sin, thus death spread to all men for all have sinned." (Rom 5:12) Death put us in captivity to the devil. "...and that they may come to their senses and escape the snare of the devil, having been taken captive by him to do his will." (2Tim2:26) "...him who had the power of death, that is, the devil."

Fortunately for us there was one over whom death and the devil's captivity had no power. Though Jesus went through death for us, paying the death demand upon our souls - it was not possible for death to hold Him because He had never sinned Himself. "Him being delivered by the determined purpose and foreknowledge of God, you have taken by lawless hands, have crucified and put to death; whom God raised up, having loosed the pains of death, because it was not possible that He should be held by it." (Acts 2:23,24) Jesus went through terrible suffering and death for each one of us - then having done everything needed for our freedom from death, God the Father raised Him to life again. In doing so He took the power of death away from the devil and reversed the tragedy of the garden of Eden. The devil was blind to what God intended to do through Jesus. "...which none of the rulers of this age knew; for had they known, they would not have crucified the Lord of glory." (1Cor 2:8)

Jesus opened the door for the power of God to flow to us. When Jesus returned from the dead the powers of darkness saw sin had been atoned for and death could be removed from every human being. The blood of Jesus received, opens the way for the Holy Spirit to enter us. Life was available to humanity again. Speaking of the coming of the Holy Spirit Jesus said," ...He will convict the world...of judgment to come...because the prince of this world is judged." (John 16:7-11) Jesus quoted Isaiah 61: 1,2 in giving the reason for the anointing of the Holy Spirit. (Luke 4:18,19) He did not include the last few words of verse 2 in Isaiah 61, but we can take it as part of God's word and it fits the context of Christs declaration. "And the day of the vengeance of our God." (against the devil)

Immediately after Christ's resurrection, when captivity was now captive, He gave gifts unto men. The gifts given all come from the one gift – the Holy Spirit. By the Holy Spirit we have gifts to enable us to enforce Christ's victory against evil in this world and to allow us to reach maturity in Godliness. The five leadership graces are called gifts, as are the graces of the Spirit to individual Christians. (Ephes 4:11,12) (1Cor 12:7)

The resurrection of Jesus means we began our new life in heaven. We are born from above. (John 3:3) Accepting Jesus as saviour means we partake in His suffering, death, burial and resurrection. "Or do you not know that as many of us who were baptised into Christ Jesus were baptised into His death? Therefore, we were buried with Him through baptism into death, that just as Christ was raised from the dead by the glory of the Father, even so we also should walk in newness of life. For if we have been united together in the likeness of His death, certainly we also shall be in the likeness of His resurrection." (Rom 6:3-5) Ephesians goes further and declares, "God...raised us up together with Him and made us sit together in the heavenly places in Christ Jesus." (Ephes 2:6) We now have the same experience Jesus spoke of when He described Himself as, "The Son of Man who came down from heaven, who is in heaven." (John 3:13) Our new born-again life began in Heaven!! We are Heavenly people having a physical experience!! That is why the New Testament calls us "Citizens of heaven." (Phil 3:20)

It is important to grasp that these truths are not just 'positional theories' but spiritual facts. Our true selves are "hidden with Christ in God." (Col 3:3) Psalm 124 gives voice to the blessedness of Christ's salvation and resurrection. With the Psalmist we can say, "If it had not been the Lord who was on our side...then they would have swallowed us alive, when their wrath was kindled against us...then the swollen water would have gone over our soul...blessed be the Lord who has not given us as prey to their teeth. Our soul has escaped as a bird from the snare of the fowlers, the snare is broken, and we have escaped. Our help is in the Lord who made heaven and earth."

SOME TIME OR ALL THE TIME?

A mentor of mine once told me of a conversation he had with a fellow Minister. The two of them were travelling speaking in churches and staying in the homes of a member of each Church. One morning they had just got on the road and my friend sensed a tension between them. The other Minister seemed to be unhappy with my friend. He asked if there was something wrong – had he done something to offend his companion? The answer was that his travelling companion had seen that he had not had a morning quiet time. He was quite upset about it – presumably because he believed they were not right with God and their ministry at the Churches would suffer. I can't recall my mentors exact answer, but I have a fair idea what he would have said.

There is certainly nothing wrong with having a morning quiet time or a time set apart to God each day. The ministers mistake was in his thinking he had made it a rule or a law. I am not right with God if I don't have a morning quiet time every day. God will be unhappy with me and my Christian life will suffer. A similar idea - if I don't spend some separate time with God daily I am starting to fall away from Him. The truth is even if I do have a quiet time or separate time alone with God daily - it doesn't come close to God's expectations of us in our relationship with Him. The implication behind these rules about time with God is that God and I are separate. He is in Heaven and I am down here, and it is my responsibility to make sure I make contact at least once a day. I can then carry on with my life secure that I have done what is required of me.

You would struggle to find much backing for that idea in the New Testament. It is more of an Old Testament concept. God was external to them and they were tasked by Him to practise external activities to keep themselves in His favour. The Old Testament is full of all the external practises required of them. Although Jesus taught often of His inner relationship with His father; "The Father who is in me He does the works" (John 5:19) "Do you not believe that I am in the Father and the Father in me?" (John 14:10) - for the disciples it was still an external relationship for most of their time with Jesus. It was only as the time for His crucifixion drew near that He began to teach them of an internal relationship for them. "The Spirit of truth whom the world cannot receive, because it neither sees Him or knows Him: but you know Him, for He dwells with you and will be in you." (John 14:17) He prayed to the Father that they might have that inner relationship. "That they all may be one, as you, Father, are in Me, and I in you; that they also may be one in Us, that the world may believe that you sent me." (John 17:21)

The change between the Old Testament relationship and the New came soon after Jesus' resurrection from the dead. "When He had said this, He showed then His hands and His side. Then the disciples were glad when they saw the Lord. So, Jesus said to them again, peace to you! As the Father has sent Me, even so send I you. And when He had said this, He breathed on them, and said to them receive the Holy Spirit. If you forgive the sins of any they are forgiven them; if you retain the sins of any, they are retained." (John 20:21-23) Suddenly they are thrust into a new inner relationship with the Father, and a responsibility to do the works of God through that relationship. God's prophecy to Jeremiah is fulfilled. "But this is the covenant I will make with the house of Israel after those days, says the Lord; I will put My law in their minds, and write it on their hearts; and I will be their God, and they shall be My people." (Jer 31:33)

More than an inner relationship – and this is my point – the disciples received a transferred life. They had become a new creation – they were now Christ people – twenty-four hours a day, seven days a week. Paul explained this life as the basic result of the Gospel. "For the love of Christ compels us, because we thus judge: that if one died for all, then have all died; and He died for all, so that all those who live may not live unto themselves, but unto Him who died and rose again for their sake." (2Cor 5:14,15) He explained his life this way, "I have been crucified with Christ: it is no longer I who live, but Christ lives in me: and the life which I now live in the flesh I live by the faith of the Son of God, who loved me and gave Himself for me." (Gal 2:20)

Certainly, it is a life to be learned. Johns Gospel in the first chapter says, "But as many as received Him, (Jesus) to them He gave the right to become the children of God, to those who believe in His name." (:12) When we first come to Jesus we are aware only of ourselves and our body. We then need to learn to become Sons of God – to learn to live in the Spirit in daily discipleship to our indwelling God. Romans 8:4 tells us "The righteous requirement of the law has been fulfilled in us who do not walk according to the flesh but according to the Spirit." We have no more laws to keep, only a relationship to be lived out. The new believer must learn to live moment by moment with God within. The goal is to enter the relationship Jesus modelled for us with His Father. "Phillip said to Him, Lord show us the Father and it will be sufficient for us. Jesus said to him, have I been with you so long and yet you have not known me, Phillip? He who has seen me has seen the Father; so how can you say, show us the Father. Do you not believe that I am in the Father, and the Father in me? The words that I speak to you I do not speak on my own authority; but the Father who dwells in me does the works." (John 14:8-10)

The believer's whole life becomes a quiet time with God. Paul called it the communion of the Holy Spirit. (2 Cor 13:14) "For as many as are led by the Holy Spirit, these are the Sons of God." (Rom 8:14) It is largely a hidden life very often not seen or appreciated by others. If Jesus inner life with His Father was not understood by those around Him, we should not expect our lives to be any different. The Minister who was upset with my friend because of his failure to have a quiet time was well off the mark.

My mentor was a spiritual man committed to a disciple relationship with God. Perhaps the Holy Spirit had instructed him to lie awake most of the night and pray. Maybe God had kept him awake and given him the message he was to speak at the next Church. The Lord might have said to him, "I want you to praise me in the Spirit for a few hours tonight."

My point is that his was a continuing relational experience with God. His only law was the "Law of the Spirit of life in Christ Jesus." (Rom 8:2) Jesus came to restore to us a Spiritual life lived in relationship with Himself, the Father and the Holy Spirit - every minute of every day.

JESUS LEADERSHIP EXAMPLE

I can't resist starting this article with a joke I saw on a baseball cap years ago. Written beneath a flustered cartoon face looking left and right was, 'I'm their leader – which way did they go?' The disciples, under Jesus' leadership, sometimes had to ask, "which way did He go"? "And in the early morning while it was still dark, He arose and went out and departed to a lonely place and was praying there. And Simon and his companions hunted for Him; and they found Him, and said to Him, "Everyone is looking for you." (Mark 1:35-37) Jesus always led from the front. One gets the sense in the Gospels of the disciples having to keep a close eye on Him to keep up with Him. I can imagine them constantly saying to one another, "Where are we going now?" Five things stand out to me about Jesus' leadership style: He led from the front - He led by example – He was constantly communicating with His team and was always available to answer questions - He kept a very close daily relationship with His Father – submission of His leadership to His Fathers will was the key to His success. Of the results of His leadership it is said: 'One Person trained twelve human beings who went on to so influence the world that time itself is now recorded as being before (BC) or after (AD) His existence.'

Laurie Beth Jones (lauriebethjones.com) a business development consultant who bases all her teaching and seminars on the leadership style of Jesus, wrote a popular leadership book. 'Jesus CEO.' (published 1995 - still available at booksellers and in Libraries) She came up with some interesting ideas after an intense study of Christs leadership in the four gospels. She talks about the Alpha leadership style – masculine authoritative - and the Beta leadership style – feminine cooperative. She says, "It struck me at the time that Jesus had many feminine values in management and that His approach with His staff often ran counter to other management styles I had both witnessed and experienced." She decided to call what she saw Jesus demonstrating - the 'Omega leadership style'. "Because His 'Omega' leadership incorporates and transcends the best of the masculine and feminine leadership styles, and by harnessing spiritual energy, each of us, female and male, can become the empowered leaders that the next millennium will require." (Written in 1995) Christs leadership example is applicable in a Christian or secular work environment.

Her book says Jesus had three vital strengths. 1.The strength of self-mastery. 2.The strength of action. 3.The strength of relationships. Every leader needs all three of these strengths and a lot of Miss Jones' consulting involves helping leaders have a good balance of these three skills. Here are some of her points for each of those strengths.

Self- mastery: Jesus developed (or in His case as the Son of God – revealed) His self-mastery by submitting Himself to a testing and training process. He was led by the Holy Spirit into the wilderness for forty days of fasting and temptation of the devil. (Luke 4:1-13)

He always spoke well of Himself. "Words have power. And Jesus always spoke loving, powerful and confident words about Himself."

"Jesus stuck to His mission." "He knew His mission statement." "In the wilderness Jesus was given several 'business opportunities' that did not relate to His mission. Each of these opportunities related to talents Jesus had, and used, in some form or another during His tenure. But He resisted them because they did not fit His mission statement."

Jesus had internal anchors. He said, "Why do you seek other people's approval but do not seek the approval that comes from only God?" (John 5:44) He was an effective leader because He had internal anchors. He did not get His approval from external mechanisms. His actions were not based on what the disciples thought. He didn't care whether Caesar smiled or frowned.

He guarded His energy. He avoided many real and potential energy leaks. He refused to engage in meaningless debates with people who only wanted to argue not learn. Even at His trial He did not waste energy on what He knew would be a meaningless defence. Jesus was so aware of His energy that once when a woman reached out and grabbed His clothes in a crowd, He turned around and asked, "Who touched me?" When they replied, "Everybody is touching you." He said. "No, I felt power go out from me." (Luke 8:45) This man was a master of the physics of energy – especially His own – and He was very careful how He used it. Jesus guarded His energy.

He did the difficult things. Leaders must have not only vision and communication skills but also tremendous personal resolve. Peter tried to stop Jesus from going to Jerusalem. He sensed danger there and he was right. However, Jesus knew it was part of a larger plan. So, He set His face toward Jerusalem even knowing the consequences. He said no, at times, to Himself. "No, I will not run from this, I will drink the cup that is placed before me." (Math 20:17-19)

Jesus saw judging others as a major energy leak. He said many times that He did not come to judge but that He came to help. He did not spend one minute on the demolition crew. He spent His energy on creation and restoration. Judging others was not His job. He said, "I do not judge you, your own words judge you." Judgment halts progress. (Luke 6:37) When we as leader's judge others we inhibit our own forward motion. Jesus reproved Peter by saying, "What business is it of yours what I say to John?" "Keep your eyes on your own forward motion." (John 21:21-23)

Strength of action: Jesus said, "My Father goes on working and so do I." (John 5:17) He asked His staff to pray for more recruits because the fields were already bursting and ripe for harvest. Things needed doing and as a leader He wanted them done – even when He knew He would not be physically present to do them. John the staff member who wrote about Him in one of the four gospels, said at the end of his story that if someone wrote down everything Jesus did the world itself could not hold the books that would have to be written. Jesus acted. She also says Jesus had a plan, He formed a team and He was bold, He broke ranks from the norm, He was willing to be visible and He put what Miss Jones calls the WOWSE concept into practise. He was going to fulfil His call 'with or without someone else.' With or without any bodies help He was going to get it done.

Strength of relationships: In His final recorded prayer on earth Jesus said. "These people were your gifts to me." (John 17:6) They were not projects to be completed, Sinners to be changed. Fools to be corrected. Worms to be transformed. Corporate pawns to be manoeuvred until the plan was in place. They were gifts to Him. Jesus beheld people. "And Jesus beheld the man and looking at him loved him." (Mark 10:21) The moment of introduction is treated as a holy moment. There is long and direct eye contact, and the leader focuses concentration on that person so that she or he feels like the most important person in the room. To behold someone means to be fully centred and to hold, or embrace, a person in that moment. The Omega leader beholds his or her people daily. People respond to how you behold them in your consciousness. You don't have to say anything, they can sense how you perceive them. Too often we only view people in terms of our needs and hidden agendas. People flocked to Jesus because He did not see them as black and white, rich or poor, male or female. He saw them as brothers and sisters – family related by blood. Equals with equal rights and responsibilities. He beheld them.

Jesus was open to people and their ideas. Why would a person with the authority and power of God go around asking people, as Jesus did, "What do you want me to do for you?" (Mark 10:51) Some think if Jesus is the Son of God He would only be telling people what to do. Not so. He was constantly asking His staff members what they were thinking and asking the people in front of Him, "What do you want?" He encouraged people to ask for things and be specific in their requests. And if God is open to our ideas, shouldn't an Omega leader be open to his or her people and their ideas. Life is about co-creation and companionship. What better way to show that than by being listening and responsive leaders. Jesus was open to people and their ideas.

Jesus empowered women. She mentions the big rise in small businesses owned by women. Jesus said to both men and women, 'The Kingdom of God is within you." He delegated equal power and authority to anyone who asked. He said in heaven there is neither male nor female, and He came to see that things were done, "On earth as it is in heaven." God spoke first to a young Mary about a magnificent plan, which she was able to keep secret until the proper time. Wealthy women financially supported Jesus and His team during their mission. (Luke 8:3) Mary Magdalene and Martha were the first to recognize the miracle of the resurrection when it happened. (Math 28:1-10) Jesus spent a lot of time with the two men on the Emmaus road and still they did not recognize him. Mary, however recognized Him almost immediately. Laurie Beth Jones is an example herself of a woman used by God in leadership for life, Church, and business. Her many books have sold in the millions and many of her clients are men wanting to know how to be better leaders. Jesus empowered women.

Jesus saw people as His greatest accomplishment. "While I was with them I was keeping them in your name which you have given me; and I guarded them and not one of them perished but the son of perdition, that the Scripture might be fulfilled." (John 17:12)

DO WE STRUGGLE FOR HOLINESS?

WORK, effort, strive, (and even) sweat, were some of the words used in an article entitled, 'Yes Holiness does require effort', in a Christian news magazine I was reading the other day. Firstly, I acknowledge that sweat was required to make Holiness available to us. Note that I have used PAST tense. Here is the sweat that was required to enable you and I to be Holy;

"And being in agony, He (Jesus) prayed more earnestly. And His sweat became like great drops of blood falling to the ground." (Lu 22:44)

The context of the words used in the article, which also included fighting, struggling, pressing, and pursuing, was self-effort. A link to another comment was entitled, Sanctification is Sweaty Work. It went on to say that, "whilst God is actively making us Holy we must also be working at it ourselves," and "we can be actively killing sin."

Have you ever tried to do those things? Waking up in the morning and deciding that today I am going to work at making myself Holy!! Today I am going to do some sin killing in me!! Where do you start? how do you know if you have succeeded? That sort of advice is meaningless when it comes to real world practise.

Also, if that advice is correct, the person who has strived the most; who has struggled more, could congratulate themselves on being a better Christian because they have put out more effort.

Some of those words are in the New Testament. For example, Jesus words in Luke 13:24, "strive to enter the narrow gate," and Pauls exhortation to "press on." Peter also tells us to "make every effort," to be partakers of the Divine nature. The Amplified Bible has Peters statement as, "make every effort to exercise your faith". And there we begin to have the true understanding of the meaning of these types of words.

Hebrews 4:1-11 holds the key to understanding the use of all these words in the New Testament. In a paradoxical statement the writer says, (:11) "Therefore let us STRIVE to enter that REST." It speaks of God's works for us being finished from the foundation of the world (:3) and that we have ceased from our own works (:10) The striving is reinterpreted as faith or belief, "let us fear lest we have unbelief." We are to strive to BELIEVE in the finished work of Jesus for us at the cross and to cease from our own works to get right with God. Holiness and a successful Christian life are a gift, through the Holy Spirit, received by faith.

That is why Colossians says, "As you have received Christ Jesus the Lord, so walk in Him."

When Jesus was asked what work was necessary to obtain eternal life, He said, "This is the work that God requires of you, that you BELIEVE in the one He has sent." (John 6:29)

A MAGNIFYING GLASS ON ROMANS 7.

Romans seven is often taken as indisputable evidence that Christians have a sin nature in cohabitation with their born-again self. After all, Paul uses the words "sin that dwells in me" twice in the chapter. He also says, "For I know that nothing good dwells in me," and "evil is present with me." End of story, right? Actually no. The truth is that conclusion does not hold water after a close look at the chapter and a comparison with Paul's other writing in the New Testament.

Before Romans seven Paul has covered in detail the just judgment of God upon sinners, the inadequacy of the law, justification by faith, the crucifixion of the old sinful self with Christ, and our rising with Him to a new spiritual life. An important aspect of our Christian life remains. That is our experience with the body which has the memory of our previous life and is dead or corrupt because of sin. The apostle begins with that subject in chapter six, focuses on it in chapter seven and adds more detail in chapter eight.

If we pay careful attention to all the phrases by Paul mentioned above, we see he was speaking about his body. Verse eighteen puts it beyond question when he says, "For I know that in me (that is, in my flesh) nothing good dwells." We could have been excused for having some doubt as to his meaning if he had not added that small explanation. Further statements in verse twenty-three and twenty-four establish the fact. "But I see another law in my members warring against the law of my mind." "O wretched man that I am! Who will deliver me from this body of death?"

His continuation of this theme in chapter eight confirms we are on the right track, "For if you live according to the flesh you will die; but if by the Spirit you put to death the deeds of the body, you will live." (Rom 8:13) Any discussion like this should factor in Pauls other writings in the New Testament.

Jesus' description of what He called "the defiled heart" in Mark 7:20-23, is the most comprehensive look at the sin nature in the New Testament. Paul is the New Testaments biggest advocate of a pure heart cleansed by Jesus' blood. It is from him we read such statements as, "To the pure in heart all things are pure," (Titus 1:15) and his description of the result in a believer of Christ's atonement, "no more consciousness of sin." (Hebrews 10:2) Only an inflexible proponent of the sin nature in the believer doctrine could hold out after so much evidence to the contrary.

It is baffling how a teaching having no support at all in the New Testament continues to be accepted by so many as the norm.

KEEPING YOUR MARRIAGE ALIVE

It might surprise you to know the Biblical book of Malachi is a great source book for marriage counselling. You could say the theme of the book is God's troubled marriage to Israel. Of course, the trouble is not on God's side. Here is Malachi 1:1 "The burden of the word of the Lord to Israel by Malachi. I have loved you says the Lord. Yet you say, 'in what way have you loved us?' You know a marriage is in trouble when one of the partners has forgotten the love that once was alive between them. God is obliged to remind them of the history of His relationship with Israel and all He had done to create a love union with them.

We often think that God's word by Malachi in 3:8-10 - "Will a man rob God? Yet you have robbed me! But you say, in what way have we robbed you? In tithes and offerings. You are cursed with a curse. For you have robbed me. Even this whole nation, Bring all the tithes into the storehouse. That there may be food in my house" - Is a rebuke to the people for not bringing their tithes to God. If we go back in the book, we find that was not the case. The people and the priests were giving tithes and offerings at the correct times under the law. The problem is revealed in 1:7-8 "You offer defiled food on my altar, but say, in what way have we defiled you? By saying the table of the Lord is contemptible. And when you offer the blind as a sacrifice, is it not evil? And when you offer the lame and sick, is it not evil? Offer it then to your governor. Would he be pleased with you? Would he accept you favourably? Says the Lord of Hosts."

God was expecting them to obey the law by enthusiastically and cheerfully bringing Him tithes and offerings of the best of everything.

Instead they were offering defiled offerings and giving the Lord animals that were of no value to them because of sickness, blindness and being lame. What has that to do with marriage? The relationship on Israel's side had broken down to a lifeless thing. They were merely going through the form of meeting the law - but the way they did that was an insult to God and an affront to His love for them. They had an attitude problem. God had expected them to keep their side of the love relationship. Instead they had allowed an attitude of deadness and rejection to creep in. They were robbing Him with defiled tithes and offerings and robbing Him of the love response He deserved.

If we look through the book we find words that are very applicable to the maintenance of a loving relationship – marriage. Honour was missing. (1:6) Reverence was missing. (1:6) The people had begun to speak contemptuously about the relationship. (1:7) They were saying, "O what a weariness this relationship is." (1:13) The fear of God was missing. (1:14) They were not taking to heart the importance of the relationship. (2:2) They had ceased to regard the word of God about the relationship. (2:6) Godly knowledge and the ways of God had been rejected. (2:7,9) They had ceased to regard the relationship as a holy institution. (2:11) Their attitude was blocking answers to their prayers. (2:13) The people had begun to despise the covenant involved in the relationship. (2:14)

God also reminds the Israelites of the many blessings that come from Him when they put effort and delight into keeping the relationship. The windows of heaven will be opened, and a blessing poured out that cannot be contained. (3:10) He will rebuke the devourer for their sakes. (3:11) They will be prosperous and people will notice they are blessed. (3:12) The Lord will look on them as His jewels. (3:17) Healing shall come to them. (4:2) Authority to trample the wicked will be given to them. (4:3)

Having absorbed the wisdom from Malachi we should now turn to the New Testament and 1Corinthians 13. We Christians have a power within us that is missing in the world. Namely the love of God. (Rom 5:5) "Now hope does not disappoint, because the love of God has been shed abroad in our hearts by the Holy Spirit who has been given unto us." 1Corinthians 13 is a description of that love in action. I have always thought one statement in the chapter is key to living in love. (Amplified Bible) "Love does not take into account a wrong done to it." In my thinking a very necessary ingredient for a successful marriage. An apostolic mentor of mine often said people come in two types. Those who are thick skinned and those who are thin skinned. Thick skinned being a metaphor for people who don't easily take offense and thin skinned for folks sensitive to rejections and wrongs done to them,

I did not want to admit it for a long time, but finally had to face that I am of the thin- skinned variety. I found that subconsciously I accumulated a list in my mind of people or organisations who were at fault in some way in regard to my values or who had done the wrong thing by me. Thin skinned out of control is no help in keeping a happy marriage. It was always a concern hovering in the back of my mind because I knew what 1Corinthians 13 said and I knew the practise of love was a major indicator of our new life. Also, there is that all encompassing verse from 2Corinthians 5:19 "That is that God was in Christ reconciling the world unto Himself, not imputing their trespasses to them, and has committed to us the word of reconciliation." The Lord has forgiven everybody in Christ. They only need to receive it. Only a few days ago I heard and saw an amazing testimony of a man who had been a violent criminal, drug smuggler and fifteen-year drug addict. By Gods mercy and patience, he came to Christ and now after only nine years is a man of love and a Prophetic leader.

I have heard it said by preachers that one word from God can change your life. I have proved that to be true. Only a short while ago God bought two words to my attention – accuse and excuse. He told me they were opposites and that excuse has the same meaning as forgive. Being a long time Christian the word forgive becomes commonplace and it takes quite a bit of mental activity to apply it to people or situations. He showed me if I said "I excuse them" it had the same meaning as forgiving. I started saying or thinking "I excuse them" to every situation that had previously disturbed me. It took two or three days to work through the subconscious list of grievances I was not fully aware I was holding. That practise brought a tremendous change and rest to my life. To make it work you need to stay alert to your responses and have a heart determination to persist. Eventually it becomes a habit and happens automatically. You have become transformed by the renewing of your mind. I strongly recommend it for married couples who have knowingly or unknowingly accumulated some offense issues in their relationship.

That leads to another basic truth of our Christian life. Colossians 3:3 puts it this way. "For you are dead and your (true real-Ampl) life is hid with Christ in God." The truth is - the part of us that takes offense and is touchy and easily hurt died with Christ at Calvary. If we take that on board as a fundamental reality of our Christian lives we will be more alert to letting our Christ selves come to the front in all our living. It is a truth that I think many Christians miss. We are not to carry on living as we did before, as singular human selves. You are dead is a strong statement. It needs meditation and commitment to accept it as a spiritual reality. God made it work for me by giving the 'I excuse' formula. He may do it differently for you. We are on a battle ground in this world and we need to succeed in getting past our humanity into the Christ life within us.

I should say also when I began applying the 'I excuse' formula it opened the way for the love and kindness and patience of God to come out in my life. I am much more tolerant of obstacles and life's petty frustrations. I notice I am more spontaneously friendly and communicative with people. I guess I should not be too surprised – to have our lives "hid with Christ in God" is an awesome and powerful reality.

DEVELOPING GODLY CHARACTER IN CHILDREN.

Hebrews chapter 12:5-11 answers some questions for us on good fathering, proper sonship, discipline, respect for parents, respect for authority and respect for God. For parents this is not a passage of do as I say but not as I do. Nobody gets off the hook in these Scriptures. Parents are to discipline their children with the same discipline God is applying to them. The whole passage is based upon the statement of verse eight. "Now if you are exempt from correction and without discipline, in which all of Gods children share, then you are illegitimate children and not sons at all." That is quite a statement when you think about it. No Christian is a Son of God without His discipline – no child in any family is a true son of that family without correction and discipline. It is a clear statement – without discipline and correction you are not sons.

I must admit here that I am not completely clear about how God disciplines us as Christians. As far as I can tell – for me anyway - it comes down to what He wants me to do and what He does not want me to do. If we are in a proper relationship with the Trinity – what the New Testament calls being led by the Holy Spirit. "For as many as are led by the Spirit of God, these are the Sons of God," (Rom 8:14) we start to experience God's plans for our lives. We should not race off and do whatever we like – we are now under God's correction, discipline and instruction – according to Hebrews 12:8. Though it may not always seem so, complete obedience to God is the place of perfect freedom. C S Lewis described Heaven as the place of perfect obedience. "The children of disobedience" is the New Testaments description of unsaved people. (Col 3:6)

It should not be left unsaid that wherever correction and discipline is mentioned in the Bible, the word love is often there also. The reason for God's correction of us is His love for us – wanting us to be all we can be. Parents correction and discipline of their children should also be out of love. The New Testament balances the message of discipline of children with Ephesians 6:4. "Fathers, do not provoke your children to anger, do not exasperate them to the point of resentment with demands that are trivial or unreasonable or humiliating or abusive; nor by showing favouritism or indifference to any of them, but bring them up tenderly with lovingkindness in the discipline and instruction of the Lord." The children's commandment is Ephesians 6:1-3 "Children obey your parents in the Lord, that is except their guidance and discipline as His representatives, for this is right – for obedience teaches wisdom and self- discipline. Honour your Father and your Mother and respect them...." Why? "That it may be well with you, and that you may live long on the earth."

God acknowledges that discipline and correction are often hard to take. We and our children are told not to lose heart because of it. (Heb 12:5) He admits it often causes sadness and is painful. (Heb 12:11) But the result is holiness and the peaceable fruit of righteousness (Heb12:11) I suspect most Christians are not sure about Hebrews 12 :5,6) "My son, do not despise the chastening of the lord. Nor be discouraged when you are rebuked by Him, for whom the Lord loves he chastens and scourges every son whom he receives." The Amplified Bible replaces 'scourge' with 'punish'. 'But Lord I have received Jesus as my Saviour. I have peace with God – now I'm to be chastened and scourged?" I think those verses reveal how much our fallen human mind fails to understand the ways of God. Anyway, we are assured that chastening is a sign of God's love, that we truly are His sons. (Heb 12: 6)

Hebrews 12 talks about the respect generated in children who have been disciplined and corrected and have been trained to submit to it. A few words in the Old Testament (1Kings 1:6) sum up the importance of correction and training of children. When King David is old, and

Solomon is about to take the throne, Adonijah, another of David's sons, plots to have himself made King. His attitude eventually leads to his death. A few words give the reason why he turned out as he did, "And his father had never reprimanded him at any time." Adonijah was a stranger to correction and discipline.

How are children taught to respect their parents and to have respect for authority? Hebrews 12:9 gives us the answer. "Furthermore, we have had human fathers who corrected us, and we paid them respect." A child without loving but firm discipline and correction has been handed a serious handicap. On the surface they may appear as everyone else but character wise they have a serious impediment. My parents were not Christians, but they were strict disciplinarians in bringing up their children. I did not like it as a child or as a teenager, but after becoming a Christian I saw they had given God something to work with in me. "Train up a child in the way he should go, and when he is old he will not depart from it." (Prov 22:6) "Spare the rod and spoil the child," (Prov 13:24) is an unpopular phrase these days. Nevertheless, there is wisdom in the instruction.

I am always interested in the background of the people God calls to do big works for Him in the earth. Always discipline and correction have played a part in making them people God can work with. Reinhard Bonke has testified that his father was very strict with his children. Some sort of arduous discipline is always found in the upbringing of these people. Smith Wigglesworth worked twelve hours a day as a young child, in agricultural work with the rest of his family. Long hours of farm work from an early age brought development of character in T L Osborn. Jesse Du Plantis does not seem to have had the benefit of a Fathers instruction, but his mother did her best to discipline her sons. That she had made her mark comes out in a story Jesse tells of his adult life before he was saved. He and his rock band were playing in a very sordid club. He was paged to come to the phone. It was his mother. Her message? "You heathen get out of that place before God kills you." He believed her. They packed up and left. Sometimes God steps in Himself when a child's upbringing has been inadequate. In Jesse's case it was a vision in his bedroom as a young boy. He says an old man with a beard came toward him out of the clouds with three words, "fear God boy!" It put the fear of God into him, which the Bible says is the beginning of wisdom. The Prophet Shepherd Bushiri was saved as a village boy. Five years of Military College before starting his public Ministry played a big part in moulding his personality and response to God.

I finish this article with a quote from the book "Who's in Charge Here?" by Dr Bob Barnes. Many young men go through an instructional time called basic training as they enter the military. It is a time of intense emotional and physical training. It is not a time as some may think to simply humiliate new soldiers. Nor is it a time to teach new soldiers to cower beneath the screams of a drill instructor. Rather, the purpose is to make new soldiers self-disciplined individuals who will be able to perform effectively in a combat situation. By putting recruits through this organised system of discipline it is hoped they will learn to avoid mistakes, and to function to their full potential and that they will be able to survive in difficult situations.

Likewise, childhood basic training helps children to develop into responsible adults who function to their full potential. The word discipline does not denote a negative form of action. A disciplinary plan is a plan that sets up boundaries for a child and allows a child to make decisions concerning those boundaries. The parent enforces the boundaries while loving the child. The child is taught to accept the consequences, rewards and responsibility for his behaviour. Responsibility is the key. The child must be placed in a position of being responsible for his behaviour. The parent must be in the position of loving the child while upholding the behavioural boundaries.

When discipline is not a basic part of a child's training it will affect their future behaviour. Lack of discipline can affect a person's vocational or professional potential. Lack of discipline can impact an individual's physical well-being and self-esteem. Lack of discipline can affect a person's ability to resist temptation. Lack of discipline can affect the stewardship of a person's possessions. Discipline or the lack of it will affect every area of a person's life.

At a very early age a child begins to test these boundaries. Not because his environment has polluted him, but because he is imperfect and self-centred like everyone else. A healthy parenting plan will establish those boundaries rather than attempt to avoid confrontation at all costs. To parent our children means that we are to prepare them for society. The world awaiting them is not devoid of boundaries and consequences. Our job as parents is to teach them about these boundaries. And that job is easier and more effective when we follow a disciplinary parenting plan that focuses on three basic concepts; responsibility, consistency and love. The responsibility for accepting his behaviour must be placed squarely on the child's shoulders. Boundaries must be set up and consistently maintained. Finally, the child must know he is loved regardless of his behaviour.

The children's commandment is, "Honour your Father and Mother." Respect is not an attitude that comes naturally to children. A parent who does not enforce a disciplinary plan is teaching a child to rebel. They are feeding the child's natural self-centeredness. It is the job of a healthy inquisitive child to rebel against the rules. It is the job of the parent to handle this rebellion with a consistent plan of loving discipline.

INTERPRETING 1 JOHN

A doctrine has been made from a few verses in 1 John 1: 7-10; "But if we walk in the light as He is in the light, we have fellowship with one another; and the blood of Jesus Christ His Son cleanses us from all sin. If we say that we have no sin, we deceive ourselves, and the truth is not in us. If we confess our sins, He is faithful and just to forgive us our sins and to cleanse us from all unrighteousness. If we say that we have not sinned, we make Him a liar, and His word is not in us."

These verses are used to support the teaching that Christians should always be confessing their sins to receive cleansing and to stay in right relationship with God. To put it another way; Christians must be preoccupied with their sins daily in order receive forgiveness and cleansing. The first problem with this teaching is that it does not consider the information in other parts of Johns letter. A discussion or conclusion is not valid unless all available information on the subject at hand has been considered.

As an example, let's take chapter 1:10, "If we say we have not sinned, we make Him a liar and the truth is not in us," and chapter 2:1, "These things I write to you that you may not sin. And if anyone sins, we have an advocate with the Father, Jesus Christ the righteous." John is giving one of his reasons for writing the letter; that his readers may not sin. If they give attention to his writing they will live without sinning. Doesn't that seem to contradict what he has just said in the previous verse? If I can live today without sinning because of John's letter does that mean that I call God a liar if I tell somebody today that I have not sinned? Also, if John is able to write a letter which can result in his readers not sinning, then to have that ability, he himself must be living without sinning. John obviously believed it was possible to live without sinning.

If we contrast other parts of Johns letter with the teaching that Christians are always sinning and needing to confess, we will find that teaching has very little support. Here is a brief list; (3:6) Whoever abides in Him does not sin. Whoever sins has neither seen Him or known Him. (3:8) Whoever sins is of the devil. (3:9) Whoever has been born of God does not sin, for His seed remains in him; and he cannot sin, because he has been born of God. (5:18) We know that whoever is born of God does not sin; but he who has been born of God keeps himself, and the wicked one does not touch him."

How then, do we interpret those first few verses in chapter 1? Talking about Jesus in 1:2,3 John says, "the life was manifested, and we have seen, and bear witness, and declare to you that eternal that was with the Father and was manifested to us—that which we have seen and heard we declare to you, that you may have fellowship with us; and truly our fellowship is with the Father and with His son Jesus Christ." He is talking to those who do not yet have fellowship with the Father and Jesus. In short, he is preaching the Gospel.

John 1:1-10 is exhortation from John to accept what God has said in the Gospel. All are sinners needing a saviour. If we say we have never sinned we make God a liar, regarding what he has said in the Gospel. If we admit that we are sinners as the Gospel says, and confess our sins, God is faithful and just to forgive us ours sins and to cleanse us by the blood of Jesus. If we say we don't need the Gospel we deceive ourselves. The Amplified Bible uses the words "truth of the Gospel" or "the message of the Gospel," three times in those verses.

One further reference outside of 1 John will help to dispel this teaching of a life of introspection for Christians. Paul gives us a brief description of his personal life with God in 1 Corinthians 4:3; "But with me it is a very small thing that I should be judged by you or by a human court. In fact, I do not even judge myself. For I know nothing against myself, yet I am not justified by this; but he who judges me is the Lord." No introspection or concern about his standing with God here. "I do not even judge myself." It is a description of a life lived in unconcerned trust in God.

JESUS ON MEN LOOKING AT WOMEN

Men need a better understanding of this statement by Jesus, "But I say unto you that whoever looks at a woman to lust for her has already committed adultery with her in his heart."

I was at a youth prayer meeting years ago, and somebody asked a Minister who was present about the meaning of this verse. My ears pricked up because I was struggling with this issue myself. He replied, "some friends of mine and I discussed this and we came to agreement that the first look is OK, and the second look is lust." Is that really the answer? Is that the best that God has for us? I don't think so.

It is important for men to think this issue through properly. We need to face the fact that we are wired to look and that the ladies are made to cause us to look! How will I know who I am attracted too and who is a potential marriage partner, if I don't look!! God put sexual attraction in us. It's not going away.

If it was not Gods intention to give us the urge so that He could delight in catching us in adultery or that we could be tormented all our lives, there must be a better solution.

The key to Jesus' meaning is in the phrases, "to lust after her" (Amplified says, with evil desire for her) and "in his heart ".

To paraphrase we could say, "He looks at her and would sleep with her if he could because of the evil condition of his heart." Christ is really talking to his listeners about the condition of their hearts. He confirmed it in Mark 7: 21 "for from within, out of the heart of men, proceed ....adulteries..." Therefore, looking is not the problem. The condition of the heart is what is important. So, what is the solution for my experience? Here it is!

The disciples received an experience on the day of Pentecost (Acts 2) that is often overlooked. Peter spoke about it (Acts 15: 8,9) "...and God gave them (the Gentiles) the Holy Spirit as He did with us........cleansing (purifying) their hearts by faith." One of the miracles of the New Testament is the pure heart obtained for us by Jesus. Does this make a difference in our looking?

Paul tells us in Titus (1:15) "To the pure in heart and conscience all things are pure." Adultery is no longer an issue.

JESUS HAD COFFEE WITH SINNERS

Jesus ate and drank with sinners, so the Gospels tell us. Probably the equivalent of our meeting at Starbucks for coffee.

A couple of days ago I read some advice to Christians for handling contact with the worlds uncleanliness. Get away from it lest you be contaminated, was the advice in brief. Is that the mind set we should have?

I don't think so. Obviously, we should not go looking for contact with the many instances of impurity in the world. We can change channels on the TV, choose not to read ugh! stuff and stay away from places exceedingly sinful if we are not going there to preach the Gospel. But what about the many situations where I can't get away. I had a situation not too long ago where I was working with a self-employed person, just the two of us together every day. He knew I was a Christian and I spoke openly about the Lord. This guy was not in the least bothered about me being a Christian and continued with his normal conversation of dirty jokes and generally off! conversation. I couldn't get away, I had to work with him for three months.

I have been in that situation many times before. It took me a while to learn, but now my first thought is always, "here is a sinner Jesus died for. He is still alive, so God is not holding his sins against him but has already forgiven him in Christ if he will accept it. Secondly, I remind myself of Mark 7:18 where Jesus says, "Are you thus without understanding also? Do you not perceive that whatever enters a man from the outside cannot defile him, because it does not enter his heart?" He goes on to say the contents of a person's heart and what comes out of it, is what defiles them. Since God has provided me with a pure heart through Jesus salvation, I don't have to be concerned about being contaminated. During that three months stint God also gave me grace to handle the situation. You do need also, to be open about being a Christian and a follower of Jesus.

It is important, and life is so much easier if we have received the pure heart that Jesus obtained for us by His suffering, death, burial and resurrection. Unfortunately, not all believers know that is available. We have read the record of an incident where Peter preaches the gospel to a group of Gentiles. The Holy Spirit is given to them and their hearts are purified by faith. The first Christians expected that to happen when the Holy Spirit turned up. Jesus also said, "blessed are the pure in heart". Speaking of the heart in Luke 6 Christ said that a good tree cannot bear bad fruit. We can therefore go out into the world knowing what God has made clean cannot be made unclean. Which allows us to focus on praying for and winning the lost to Christ.

WE WIN IN HIM

Many years ago, I had an experience I believe was allowed by God to teach me an important lesson in dealing with our spiritual enemies. I was a team member of a street outreach ministry in Auckland, New Zealand. My responsibility was to mingle with the people listening to the Preacher. When I thought it appropriate I would ask individuals what they thought of the message and try to engage them in a gospel conversation. One afternoon very few people were listening, and I decided to try for a conversation with people passing by. A man of about 60yrs, in working gear, walked through. I approached him and asked if he knew Jesus had died for his sins. I got more than I bargained for when he turned to me and said, "Son, you say one more word to me and I will knock your head off."

I was contemplating how to respond to that when suddenly I became aware of an evil spiritual force rising off him. To me it seemed about nine or ten metres high. Along with it was the realisation the flesh and blood me was powerless against such a thing. In an instant another change happened as I saw a shimmering spiritual circle replace the evil spirit. I knew it was from God. It came down from above and encircled both of us. It gave peace to me, and the man turned abruptly and walked off. I was a relatively new Christian at the time, and that experience warned me I was never to engage the enemy in my own strength. I was a zealous young evangelistic Christian always looking for chances to preach the gospel. Perhaps God could see that in the future I would get myself into trouble, and he stepped in and gave me an important lesson.

I think it is significant we have only three references to warfare in the New Testament. 2 Cor.9:7 refers to provision for Gospel preachers. 1Tim 1:18 is Paul instructing Timothy to have faith in the prophecies spoken to him to ensure success in his Christian life. Here Paul refers to Christian living as, "the good warfare." In the next verses he equates having faith as waging a good warfare. The third reference, 2 Cor 10:1-5, has a lot to teach us regarding the notion of the Christian life as warfare, "Now I Paul, myself am pleading with you by the meekness and gentleness of Christ – who in presence am lowly among you, but being absent am bold towards you. But I beg you that when I am present I may not be bold with that confidence that I intend to be bold against some, who think of us as if we walked according to the flesh. For though we walk in the flesh, we do not war according to the flesh. For the weapons of our warfare are not carnal but mighty in God for pulling down strongholds, casting down arguments and every high thing that exalts itself against the knowledge of God, and bringing every thought into captivity to the obedience of Christ..."

Here, first, is Biblical backing for the lesson God taught me mentioned above. Paul says he is meek and gentle and lowly among them. Though he walks in the flesh he does not war in the flesh. He does not run about as a demon chaser. The record in Acts 19: 13-16 of some non-Christian Jews who decided to deal with demons in their own strength, should be a warning to us. "Then the man in whom the evil spirit was leaped on them, overpowered them, and prevailed against them, so that they fled out of that house naked and wounded." Paul takes his refuge in God for a winning Christian life. "The weapons of our warfare are not carnal (fleshly) but mighty in God." We have more insight on these issues in Jude 1:9. "Yet Michael the archangel, in contending with the devil, when he disputed about the body of Moses, dared not to bring a reviling accusation, but said, 'The Lord rebuke you." Michael joins Paul in taking refuge in the Lord in dealing with spiritual evil.

The 2 Corinthians passage continues with the 'not in the flesh' theme by revealing the victorious Christian life has everything to do with our thinking. The winning Christian rejects carnal fleshly thinking and instead brings all his thought processes into captivity to Christ. He lives his life, "In Christ." In telling us to go and serve Him, Jesus said, "All power and authority is given unto me, in heaven and on earth." (Math 28:18) Yes, we have power and authority, and it is found in Him. The 2 Corinthians passage also refers to the power and authority we have in Christ to influence the minds of unbelievers. This how the living Bible puts it: "It is true I am a weak ordinary human being, but I don't use human plans and methods to win my battles. I use God's mighty weapons, not those made by men, to knock down the devil's strongholds. These weapons can break down every proud argument against God and every wall that can be built to keep men from finding Him. With these weapons I can capture rebels and bring them back to God and change them into men whose heart's desire is obedience to Christ." If ever there was a Scripture to make our own, by faith, it is those words.

Jesus told us to go into all the world but said our power and authority for that task was in Him. Paul was the most aggressive gospel Minister, yet he said I don't do it in the strength of my humanity. "I worked harder than all the others, but it was not me but the Grace of God that is in me." (1Cor 15:10) It is a fair question to ask, "how do I do that"? "How do I know I am in Christ and His strength when I go?" The answer is twofold. By faith in the Word of God and the development of a relationship with God the Father, the Lord Jesus Christ and the Holy Spirit. Only one person has power and authority over demons and that is the Lord Jesus. The New Testament says we are, "to be found in Him." (Philip 3:9) An aggressive Christian life comes by faith in the Word and close relationship with God triune. Jesus our example, declared while on earth, He did nothing of Himself but only that which came forth from His relationship with His Father. (John 5:30-32)

Most of the New Testaments guidance to us regarding dealing with evil spiritual enemies is stated as resistance. Our resistance is founded on the fact that Jesus defeated the devil through His death, burial, resurrection, and the shedding of His blood on our behalf. "For this purpose, was the Son of God manifested that He might destroy the works of the devil." (1John 3:8) "In as much then as the children have partaken of flesh and blood, He Himself likewise shared in the same, that through death he might destroy him who had the power of death, that is the devil." (Heb 2:14) Though we have already won in Christ we still live in an environment where the devil goes about like a roaring seeking some to devour. "Be sober, be vigilant; because your adversary the devil walks about like a roaring lion, seeking whom he may devour. Resist him, steadfast in the faith, knowing that the same sufferings are experienced by your brotherhood in the world." (1Peter 5:8,9) 'Therefore submit to God. Resist the devil and he shall flee from you." (James 4:7)

Paul tells us why we need the armour of God (Ephesians 6) in verses 11, 13, 14. "that you may be able to stand" "that you may be able to withstand" "stand therefore." These phrases have the same meaning as resist. And how are we to stand and resist? "Be strong in the Lord and the power of His might." (Ephes 6:10)

To finish, I want to share something the Lord showed me recently. I have known for a long time that I can exercise authority in Christ when I encounter opposition from spiritual evil. I had a tendency when doing that to put a lot of emotional and physical energy into it. I thought I needed to raise my voice, possibly even shout when commanding evil to go. I think many Christians feel the same way. After many years as a Christian, the Lord, one day, put the thought into my mind that the Gospels show Jesus dealing with demons with just a word. "When evening had come, they brought to Him many who were possessed by demons. And He cast out the spirits with a word and healed all that were sick." (Math 8:16)

The Lord asked me, "which is the bigger manifestation of faith, putting a lot of human energy into it or using just a word?" I caught on immediately. Jesus had the strongest faith in His own authority. He knew He had only to speak a single word of command as the Son of God, to make the demons obey. If I am in Christ, and the word tells me I am, I am exercising the strongest faith when I also speak just a word or short command to evil spirits. God's power is released through us by faith. I, then, need to use the strongest path of faith to apply full power against my enemy. I challenge you to try it. Use a word or short command and stick to it by faith. You will be surprised by the results.

https://www.hebten.blogspot.com

THE END

About the Author

Ross Thompson lives in Melbourne Australia. He is semi-retired after many years of full time and part time involvment in Pastoral and Evangelistic ministry. He was also a Bible college lecturer and has some Theological qualifications. Presently he uses his teaching gift to write for the edification of anybody interested in Christianity and Christians.

Read more at https://www.amazon.com/author/rossthompson.

www.ingramcontent.com/pod-product-compliance
Lightning Source LLC
Chambersburg PA
CBHW020526030426
42337CB00011B/564